I0426317

A MESSAGE TO THE UN-AMERICAN

Florentino Prieto Azuar

Suzanne Prieto Berry

Copyright © 2012 Author Name

All rights reserved.

ISBN: 1493782584
ISBN-13: 9781493782581

DEDICATION

I dedicate this book to my late father, Florentino Prieto Azuar, who continues to inspire me to appreciate the "American Dream".

CONTENTS

INTRODUCTION

In 1945 my father had a burning desire to express the gratitude he felt for having lived the American Dream. He had all the set backs that would preclude him from achieving a successful and fruitful life
had he not stepped on board a steam boat, thrown his Puerto Rican
sombrero to the wind and taken the plunge of opportunities that only
America could offer. As his daughter, and fortunate enough to have been born under the fruits of his successful labors, I too have felt compelled to deliver his message of gratitude which unfortunately
our beloved USA has been taken advantage of, likened to a society
of spoiled teenagers. This is the story of that American Dream, which one questions today, how sustaining that enigma might be?!
My father was born in the small town of Rincón, Puerto Rico. His parents were of

meager means and had six children to raise. No one knows why only My father not only had the desire, but fortitude to persevere and go against what could have been his card in life. All his brothers and sisters settled for the path of least resistance. It was not uncommon in the small territorial island of Puerto Rico to set one's self apart from the United States just as teenagers often rebel against their parent's good intentions. My father was the anomaly, although in his days of youth, he adhered to the mass opinions of having Puerto Rico succeed on it's own, and being an "independista;" remaining stagnant with no successful future in site, began to nag at my father with a vengeance. After all, he had what it took to make it in America –desire. Not withstanding his meager background and incredibly thick Spanish accent, less than lily white skin, perseverance and an old battered valise eventually made his dreams come true. With those more than obvious set back, my father graduated with honors from Valparaiso University School of Law, located in Indiana, and proudly returned to his beloved island to set his dream in motion. Americanized he was. Not only did he marry an American, but a Jewish American which seemed an outright rebellion to his mother and sisters whom he financially and respectfully supported for years.

My brother and I were born in the fifties. To say we had every material comfort life could offer, was an understatement. Mother never had to work, let alone participate in much child rearing as we had a Nanny, a cook, a daily cleaning woman and an ironing lady. If my father prided himself in being married to what solidified his stature in being fully Americanized, my mother certainly was the recipient of that good fortune.

Life was idyllic, thanks to my father's belief that one could climb out of the shackles of poverty, where his children were afforded every material and educational opportunity he,--almost did not. But because of the opportunities that Uncle Sam presented everyone just

for the asking, life in the United States of America was indeed the land of opportunity. Although my brother and I reaped every accoutrement our growing
years presented us, it wasn't until after my father passed, did I begin to question whether our American Dream passed with him. I was one of the fortunate few, I went through college, studied abroad, was able to travel extensively –all on the wings of my father's dream. Unlike today where most college students cannot afford their education and must work one, and sometimes two jobs in order to make a career – let alone a living! Admittedly it is tougher today. More homes than not consist of a two working parent family, where latch key kids are left alone to microwave tv dinners; one wonders whatever happened to home
cooked meals and the stability of sitting down together?
Although America has been wounded, I and my father are one of
many that will never give up the dream that our forefathers
heroically laid the path for our future generations to come.

I recall growing up in the 70's where the hippy movement felt like
teenagers rebelling on a societal level, the breakdown of our great
country. It is every parents hope that once teenagers get their
rebellious nature out of their system, they will come to their senses
and realize that they had it pretty darn good – after all.
Fast forward to 911, and our country under a microscope looks as if
the cancer of our naïve hippy teenage years has metastasized like a
cancer that runs rampant it's rage of destruction.
What has happened to our American Dream is what I feel so
compelled to give my father's words –a voice.
Has my father's America become too lenient, too soft; did we let our
children and most importantly our all too generous hand outs to
foreigners --bite the hand that fed them!?!
Since 911 there have been numerous and all too many vicious

attacks against our beloved, land of the free. It is a double edged

sword. We and our soldiers have continually paid the supreme

sacrifice so that we can continue living in freedom, but because I

feel helpless, like so many law abiding American citizens to stop the

carnage against this still great nation, this is why I feel compelled to

dust off the musty cover of my late father's manuscript and reveal it's

ingenuous and altruistic cry for help. A cry for help that may

resonate a ripple effect for what our children and their children must

come to appreciate in order to stand up against an inoperable fight.

I hate to imagine the sadness and disbelief that would come over my

father if he were alive today, knowing that the dream he so

poignantly wrote about was being destroyed by the very generous

hand of opportunity that was given to him. How dare we invite with open arms, foreigners that claim to deserve

the same equal rights all Americans have, but to turn around and set
off explosive bombs killing innocent men, women and children after
we've opened up our doors of opportunity to them.
What started out as the giving and forgiving patriarch to foreigners
who masked a genuine need, got blown in our face and it's no longer
our heroic soldiers that are fighting for our freedom, but our
innocent men, women and children that no longer walk the streets
with abandon.
If terror be what the terrorist want in order to break our spirits, we
need to stop being so altruistic and forgiving and crack open our
history books in order to learn what our father's knew when they
cracked the whip in order to allow us to appreciate what we have.
We are still a great nation, hopefully not standing by a string. There

is always hope, and strong leadership. Like the one's my father grew
up with from Truman to Reagan, is what I've no doubt my father
would agree that we ever so much need today. My father worked hard for his degree; he washed dishes and took on
various jobs that would allow him to become a respectful and
honorable citizen in the country he loved. Today, too many people blame this great country for what amounts
to pure laziness and I dare say it is our soft government with it's all
too generous hand outs that has crippled this nation.
Today the Florentino's that came to this country with a suitcase full
of books has been replaced with foreign zealots with suitcases full of
bombs!
We've progressively been living under a deep sleep. An occasional
terrorist attack allows us a momentary sense of high alert, but when
will this country wake up out of it's coma?

I share my father's story because it is one of many stories that may

spark a glimmer of hope, to the way we were; to the way we could

be again. We are a strong and determined people. Our diversity is

the fulcrum of what makes us unique and strong.

We don't have to come from an impoverished situation to be

successful in America, but in spite of whether we do, the

opportunities afforded us with the good work ethic this country was

founded on, are like the similar roots of my father, that in which we

need to recall and embrace once again.

My father's story was written in 1945. It's a simple heartfelt account

of desire and appreciation; this I believe is fundamental in getting

this country back on it's feet. We don't need to be crippled by a

government that indiscriminately hands out free passes to the

immigrant, the underdog, or the terrorist that falls under those same
liberal rights.
I'm not saying that people don't deserve to be given a chance, but
that indiscriminate hand outs ARE what are undermining our
country. It has weakened our backbone and "weakness" in the wild
kingdom is always the fallen prey.
If I can take from my father's example, what he taught me was that
perseverance and sheer determination, along with gratitude and
religious belief are what make you a respectable human being. I
personally believe that through your faith in your God, cumulatively,
we can awaken this great nation –back out of it's flat line.
I would also like to add, that my father's heart felt story is still one of
many. I wanted to bring his story to the public –especially today
since every, and any bit of hope --DOES keep us alive.

This, is my father's message:

A MESSAGE TO THE UN-AMERICAN

THROUGHOUT this message I am going to address you, foreigners
and anti-Americans from all corners of the world, with the
earnestness, I should say, of an improvised soap-box speaker
somewhere along colorful Columbus Center in New York City. Of
course, the place of my choice does not really matter. I might as
well be addressing you all from a makeshift stand in Chicago's Little
Italy or somewhere along the Windy City's tough and heterogeneous
South Side or even from Galveston's or Albuquerque's Mexican
quarters. The important thing is that this heart-felt message reach
you wherever you are, it being utterly immaterial what the color of

your skin is or what, if any, your religious belief may be. And if
there is any "ism" attached to your political ideology, which may be
in conflict with the American democratic creed and the American
way of living, come forward and listen to me. Again, if you are
among the chosen ones allowed to emigrate to this country, or if you
belong in the so-called persecuted races or peoples of the world, or if
you are one among the unheard of and forgotten little men, get
forward and listen to me! And even if you are a gangster or an
outcast or an ex convict or a parolee and feel that you have lost your
social and legal standing among your fellow citizens this side of the
Atlantic, I also have a word for you.
This message is not a sermon or a panacea for your social or political
troubles. It is a bare statement of facts based on observation and

experience. It is said that when we are too close to the woods we
fail to see the trees. Even hundreds of thousands, millions perhaps,
of native-born Americans constantly fail to get a real grasp on the
grandiose achievements of their forefathers who built up a nation
from coast to coast with their bare hands, and their myopic
indifference definitely makes them lose track of what is really going
on around them in a world which is constantly changing precisely
due to the tremendous and united efforts of the individuals of their
own generation. In deed they fail to see the imponderable charm
behind that most graceful of all-American institutions, the hot-dog,
as well as the scientific import of the atomic bomb which wrestles
from God's own hands His up-to-now unchallenged power to create
and rule the worlds!
If many an American is adamant to the great potentialities around

him, if he is unaware of the creative genius of his fellowmen, of the
vastness and richness of the land on which his forefathers set foot; if
her has forgotten all about the deep-set mysticism of the Pilgrim
Fathers, whose romantic adventure for once betrays the hastily
accepted legend of the American greed for gold and things material;
if he does not care for the epic gesture of the men and women who
went West in their screeching covered-wagons , challenging
voracious beasts and Indians but rolling up the horizon until they
were stopped by the Pacific Ocean only to add up to the azure of
their invincible flag, originally clustered by thirteen stars, a
portentous constellation of forty-eight undimmed stars; if he has
forgotten these traditions which are the very marrow of the history of
his fatherland, I want to bring them up to you, citizens from all lanes

of this aging world saturated with post-war frustrations, so that you
may have faith and hope in America –a living beacon among the
decadent nations of the world!
I would be too contented, though I realize it is quite pretentious, if
this message were translated into your own language, whether you
are German or Japanese or Nordic or Hottentot, so that you may
understand in your own unbiased thinking the little as well as the
important things about which I am going to discourse.
This message of mine has lived in my brain for many years. Some
one has said one is not a man if he has not achieved one of three
things, namely, have a child, plant a tree or write a book. I am still,
hopelessly it seems, a bachelor, and have not planted a tree nor
written a book. The itch for the latter has been unbearable, and,
although I originally intended to publish it in a newspaper, I feel that

with its publication in book form, I am paying America a tribute of
deep-felt gratitude.
But perhaps it was for the better that I should wait all these years to
write down my message since considerable travel throughout many
States of the Union has put me in better contact with things
American. Among those States I have visited, I recall Florida,
Georgia, the Carolinas New Jersey,
Pennsylvania, Ohio, Indiana,
Illinois, Missouri, Kentucky, Tennessee,
Louisiana and Texas, and,
of course, Puerto Rico, the territory of my birth. Among these, I
love the Hoosier State best, for I studied law in Valparaiso, which
typifies the American village in the stock of it's population and in its
unsophisticated atmosphere. Besides, Indiana is perhaps the most
American of all the States for, being almost the geographical heart of

the nation, it was crisscrossed by pioneering caravans during frontier
days and the red blood and demeanor of its settlers has not change to
this day.
I still can visualize the typical American farmer on a hot summer day
sitting on one of the benches outside the county court in dear old
Valparaiso; tall and muscular, with a blond wavy beard and hayscented
dungarees, chewing his eternal tobacco plug and hollering at
his neighbors a congenial "Howdy!" An exact personification of
Uncle Sam as I have always imagined him!
I regret that something of an autobiography will have to be
interwoven in this message, but it is only to bring home to you in a
more factual way the aim and goal behind this work.
For all that matters I might have been born anywhere outside the
United States, with a different vernacular, a different religious creed

and a different racial ancestry. And so it was indeed, for I was born
in the village of Rincón, in the tiny Island of Puerto Rico and
Spanish is my native tongue.
At the age of eighteen I graduated from high school and although I
was taught some notions of the English language now I realize that
at that time I made myself understandable only with the help of my
hands and my all-Latin gestures. I was born and raised in a truly
middle-class atmosphere, the smallest of four brothers and two
sisters.
My father struggled as a light-house keeper to give us at least a
common school education and some of us went beyond the eighth
grade. I was by far the most ambitious and always cherished dreams
of a profession, but father's salary could hardly take care of the
grocery bills. So, when I obtained my high school diploma my

dreams of a career had seemingly collapsed. I remember too well
that while every one in my graduating class felt very happy about the
event, the idea that I might never get a more dignified sheepskin
mortally depressed me. We celebrated the occasion in a public
restaurant with toasts and cheers, but I felt terribly unhappy
nevertheless. I could already see in my imagination most of my
well-to-do school mates turned into doctors and lawyers while it
would be my sad fortune to work somewhere as a humble clerk or
even be bossed by my graduating chums. Unlike the American teenager, the Puerto Rican adolescent,
descendant of the quixotic conquistadores, goes more for the serious
and even tragic things of life or at least he thins he does, and he does
his best to live up to that sophisticated standard. The same is also
true with every South American teenager; indeed, with every

teenager the world over except the United States. We shall presently
see how utterly nonsensical and psychologically harmful the moral
pose and attitude of the boys below the Rio Grande is; and I hope
that you and I and our grandchildren will instead forever envy and
admire the honesty and simplicity and resourcefulness of
Huckleberry Finn and thus at least atone for the immature venality of
our Pepés and Panchos.
While the average American boy is foot-ball minded and does not
care much for books and literature outside his curriculum, it is a
must with our Latin boys to write poems and deliver speeches. It is
in their blood that they will eventually dominate multitudes and
master the destiny of their countries, or at least they so expect.
Time, however, has taught us a bitter lesson to the contrary. The

sum total of this premature waste of energy and of this most
improper channeling-in of would-be talent is the legions of mediocre
tyrants and greedy lawyers that rule our countries snuffing out our
very lives and our unlimited potentialities.
So I took to writing at an early age. Or was it writing? I distinctly
remember that a kind editor published my first rhymed prose –a stuff
loaded with moon and swans—at the tender age of fifteen. From
then on I deluged the local papers and magazines with all sorts of
poems and essays on most every conceivable subject. So at 18 my
name was well publicized along my native Island and I felt that I
was sitting on top of the literary world! Yes, O yes, I must enter then
the political arena. And so I did by delivering inflammable speeches
on behalf of our political independence.
I had all the weapons at hand to make myself a famous man: the

stampede of my oratory and writer's name. Of course, I did not

possess a college degree, but many a famous man had not gone

through a university and still I was only 18 years old.

I must make clear that at that time I honestly and sincerely believed

that the best course for my little country to follow was to sever all

connections from Uncle Sam and become a free republic. And even

at present I still think that should the United States question the right

deserves of our citizenship there is no other choice for my people but

to peacefully fight for their independence. Yet there is and there will

always be a secret longing in my heart for things American and I

sincerely hope that the friendly bonds that have always tied us to the

United States shall never be severed.

I regret to say that at the age of 18 I was not exactly Un-American,

but anti- American. I dreamed of the day when the stars and stripes
gave way to our lone-star flag. And I wrote poems and continued
making speeches about the all-absorbing subject of our national
independence. At that time I nursed real contempt for American
books, for American soldiers, for American institutions, for my own
American citizenship which I then thought was hastily canned by a
war congress (1917) as a bait to induct us into the army. How wrong
I was, although many of my countrymen still follow that unfortunate
trend of thought! If they could only cross the ocean, as a nation, and
see things here for themselves!
In my travels I have met many young folks from South America and
most of them, especially those from Mexico, the Dominican
Republic, Colombia and Nicaragua, are still contemptuous of Uncle
Sam. In fairness to factual truth, it cannot be denied that their

grudge is not merely fanciful for they cannot forget even today the

merciless territorial slashing of the Aztec Republic, the ungrounded

intervention of the Hispaniola, the grabbing of the Panama Canal

Zone through the irresistible big-stick policy of Teddy Roosevelt

nor the mowing-down of the Sandino followers. The embittered

genes of their forefathers are ever present in them for while they

belong to a race that easily forgives they cannot easily forget.

Something must really be done to induce them to bury their hatchet

and I dare suggest that through international amicable channels the

undeniable American virtues and institutions be propagandized in

the shape of a short course to be taught in the public schools south of

the Rio Grande and this country could reciprocate the good neighbor

gesture by similarly teaching its school- going generation that down there not every thing is bad hombres and tequila.

On board the S.S. Macori's I met once a young chap from Santo
Domingo, verging on the 20's. I was then 27 and I struck a
conversation with him. He was well-to-do and had left his native
country to make up a career, and, apparently to conquer the world.
He told me he was going to study medicine at Heidelberg, but upon a
swift and polite cross-examination I found out that he had no
knowledge of the German language and that his prep-school was
tantamount to a grammar school education. He was, however,
polished in his manners and refined in his diction. Although I was
barely seven years his senior, I at once mentally established the
similitude between his bombastic reasoning and expectations and my
own line of thinking when I was his age. Like me, he had also

acquired a literary name in his native country by writing poems in
the Dominican papers and by delivering occasional speeches there.
With that intellectual baggage he expected to storm his way through
ancient Heidelberg ---even though he did not possess an elementary
scientific backing for the pursuit of his chosen career. I could not
help but pity him, for that was exactly the way I thought and acted
less than a decade before.
Yes, that is the trouble with our Latin youngsters. That young chap
from Santo Domingo typifies them all. WE think we know too
much when we are 18, and, what is worse, many of us think that we
are geniuses past the curve of 40.
I have met many American students of both sexes while in college
and only recently when I visited my Alma Mater for two consecutive
years, and they certainly react in a different way. They are simple,

unsophisticated, amiable and morally disciplined, and, above all,

they are true to their age. Any American college boy is clean-cut

and unpretentious. He is happy if he makes up his grades, dates a

girl once in a while and goes to a foot-ball or basket-ball game

whenever he can. And, of course, give him chewing gum and an

average picture show and he will feel too contented.

Most of the South American students, and I know it for a fact, think

that the average American student is simply bore-some and silly.

They find him childish. It is a pity that so many South American

students never finish up their studies when they come to this country

and thus miss the opportunity of knowing intimately his Northern

neighbors.

When it gets to mixing and knowing each other during the first days

of their acquaintanceship, the youngster from the South is hopelessly

bored by the youngster from the North. Take for instance two
youngsters 18 years of age in their first year of college. Call it
blood, race or tropical heat, the fact is that at that tender age the boy
from the South looks and acts like a man about town, while his
Nordic counterpart is still bent on his marbles, at least morally
speaking. The former will at once indulge in skid row conversation
while the latter simply gapes at him, and, instead of being favorably
impressed with tales about the oldest profession on earth, with
concealed disgust he slowly but surely changes the conversation to
the Cards or the Red Sox or to the motor trouble he is having with
his jumping jalopy. Or the American boy will invite his Southern
neighbor to go to church the coming Sunday, an invitation which
needless to say will be declined with roaring laughter.

The astounding difference between the behavior of the two given
adolescents may be a problem to be taken up by the psychologist but
in my opinion it is, above all, a problem of painstaking re-education.
The American boy is taught since his early childhood to go to church
and he grows up to be a God-fearing citizen while the Latin fellow's
Christian education is altogether neglected by his parents. In fact, a
boy 18 will be called a sissy by his companions if he is caught
coming out of church South of the border. The church, in their
opinion, is good stuff for their sisters and kid brothers, but not for
them who at the age of 18 may already have had a paramour and no
doubt have already made the nocturnal rounds of the wild spots.
This may sound astounding to the average good- natured American
reader but it is just as I say, with perhaps isolated exceptions, all the
way from Mexico to Patagonia.

The Latin boy since his early puberty is completely sex-minded.
You can find him in any picture show, after the lights are out, avidly
moving from seat to seat until he finds a girl or woman with whom
to rub knees in subdued desperation. No wonder many an
experienced American woman frankly longs for the Latin type! The
American boy, on the contrary is satisfied with merely holding hands
in rather a friendly way and does not mind double dates, a thing
abhorred by the Latin youngster who craves for privacy. And fi the
American boy is alone in a picture house he will simply stretch out
his big feet and relax body and soul without losing a detail of the
picture before his eyes.
How I pursued my studies in America is quite a long story. As soon
as I obtained my high school diploma, with a salutatorian award, I

got a job as a stenographer in one of the government agencies in San
Juan. I despised it for still I wanted to become a lawyer. My parents
could not afford to send me to college and I could not give up my
job with which I helped them out. Nevertheless I wanted to find a
decent way out without letting them know that I was quitting my
work.
So one day I wrote a terrific article in a local newspaper calling the
Governor, an American appointee, a carpetbagger and the like. But
since it was written in Spanish, I did not hear from His Excellency.
It seems that all my plans had come to nothing, but again, I had
another idea. This time I enclosed the newspaper clipping in an
envelope addressed to the Governor, without a return address, and
scribbled on the clipping that the author was working in such and
such department. Tow days after I received a short letter from the

chief executive informing me that "for the good of the service" my
position had been eliminate.
Was I glad with the news? Indeed I was, for that official re script
definitely changed the course of my entire life!
My mother, truly the Latin type, was all tears when I conveyed to her
the "Sad" news of my predicament. "You'll have to find yourself
another job, Son," she told me in desperation. "Oh no," I said to
myself. Much as though I loved my mother, this time I was not
going to gamble against my future! I had saved around $300
precisely for this big occasion and if my parents were unable to
defray my studies, all I needed was enough money for a steamer
ticket, a second-hand overcoat and a down payment on my tuition
fee.
So the day arrived when I should get ready to sail away and leave

my Island and my folks for the first time in my life. My mother was
sobbing all the time while my father and brothers and sisters shed
furtive tears. Had they truly been American folks they would no
doubt have wished me good luck and kept talking about the near
future when I would return with my "abogado's"(law) degree. But
instead of cheering me up my mother kept on saying, with the inborn
pessimism of our race, that she would not live to see me again. That
is always the way with Latin hearts, and that truly sickened me to the
marrow of my bones. But fortunately she did live to see me get back
with my lawyer's degree and I know that she has ever since been
very happy about it all.
I don't deny that I felt as though I had left my whole heart behind
me, and that the sight of my little island from the deck of the ship
was all too unbearable to me. Besides, the ship was crowded with

sophomore and senior smarties, scions of
well-to-do families who
returned to the States for their fall courses.
Their nifty suits,
compared to my baggy pants, seemed just
retrieved from Esquire's.
I noticed then, while leaning on my elbows,
that the roaring
pretenses of my philosophical 18 years were
going a shambles under
the impact of that irrepressible melancholy
which only the ocean,
with its grandiose symphony, casts onto our
wavering hearts.
During my entire life I have kept to myself as
far as I have been able
to and have never been much of a mixer. That
is why I did not feel
quite at ease amidst that bunch of boisterous
students who seemingly
knew their way around the big American
cities. I felt like a hill-billy
among them and a sensation of self-frustration
overpowered me.
While we were already losing sight of the
palm tress and the evergreens

of my native isle, and before I knew what it was all about,
one of the students tossed my straw-hat into the ocean. "You won't
be needing that thing anymore," he told me while the other fellows
broke into roaring laughter. I guess there was a silly smile on my
face when I saw my poor old hat glide away into the foamy sea.
I hated those fellows from the bottom of my heart. I thought they
were brainless and foolish. But the march of time has taught me
differently. On the contrary, I now realize that they were goodnatured
and game, congenial and unspoiled. They had already
assimilated the simple and graceful attitudes of the typical American
boy, while I, not conversant with the new life and ways ahead of me,
still remained taciturn and biased.
The joyous crowd finally dispersed in New York City while I
remained all alone at the foot of the pier, gaping at the far-off

monumental structures. Push carts with pyramidal heaps of

suitcases and black porters seemed to come from all directions and I

had to keep on moving and jumping sideways to avoid being overrun

or stepped over. Then there came a red-cap hollering at me, "Check,

mister, check!" And before I realized what it was all about, he

grabbed my trunk (mind you a trunk), leaving in my shaking hand

what seemed to me a silly piece of paper. I stood there several

minutes motionless and speechless.

Well, that was that! And now, little man, what next if you know, I

asked myself with a silly smile. Suddenly I caught sight of the last

student to depart, a senior, who was engaging a taxi. I pleaded with

him to let me get into his cab, very well realizing that I did not know

where I was going to. And my dear fellow country-man just brushed

me away, New York fashion, slamming the
door on my very nose! I
don't know where I managed to draw courage,
but all that I now
remember is that in my utter defenselessness
and desperation I
jumped through the other door and found
myself practically on the
fellow's lap.
He went to an apartment house somewhere on
Third Avenue and, no
telling, I stuck by him as though to my
mother's apron strings.
Fortunately for me, the hostesses, a couple of
Puerto Rican spinsters,
some how got fond of me and they showed me
the town from the top
of a double-decker. I confess I was dazed at
the sight of the
skyscrapers and of the crowds of "the
sidewalks of New York."
But who wouldn't, after all?
"What a people!," I said to myself, "What a
country!"
I envied the Puerto Rican fellow who in that
stupendous cathedral of

massive mortar and steel called the
Pennsylvania Station managed to
find his way around and made the necessary
arrangements, in perfect
English, for my trip to the Middle West and
even placed me on the
proper gate amidst the roar of incoming and
outgoing trains in what
seemed to me a veritable replica of Dante's
inferno.
I remember it too well now. It was a 17th of
September during the
roaring twenties. Yet I was already wearing
my second-hand
overcoat inside the train coach. An elderly
lady was sitting by my
side and in my great fear of the unknown
ahead, I must have looked
to her much younger than my 18 years, for she
kept on smiling at me
and even tried to start a conversation.
But, mark my words, I did not understand a
thing of what she was
telling me, notwithstanding my high school
diploma! Back in my

native island I thought it was patriotic to ignore and even forget all

notions of the English language – the tongue of our oppressors. Of

course, without admitting how foolish I had been with my past

behavior, I felt then as though I would have given anything in the

world to make that kindly lady's acquaintanceship. I wonder who

she was and what she may be doing now if she is still alive. She was

the first amiable soul I met in this country and the lapse of years will

never efface her kindly smile nor the warmth of her blue yes from

my aging heart! Have you ever met a perfect stranger on a bus, or a

train, or a plane, be it of your own or of the opposite sex, to whom

for unexplainable but alive psychological reasons you have felt

yourself deeply attached? Didn't you feel as though you knew that

person for ages, perhaps in an abstract and mysterious world beyond

the scope of all human understanding, and haven't you deeply
regretted that the end of your journey was also the end of your casual
friendship? Well, that happened to me that cold autumnal evening,
although at the time I was not fully aware of the psychological
changes that were overcoming me.
Needless to say, I could not afford the luxury of a private
compartment nor of a Pullman reservation. So, like a child, I kept
poking my nose against the glass window, trying in vain to peep at
the moving things through the stillness of the heavy night.
When my train arrived in Philadelphia I noticed sudden jolts and
jerks and then the train remained still. It didn't look to me like an
ordinary train stop, but rather like the end of my journey. Then I saw
a few women come up to my coach and sweep it rather leisurely.

And then lots of new passengers got on board and set their luggage
as best they could. And the train started moving again, slowly
screeching at first and finally roaring and bouncing over its winding
tracks. So that was it! I really got panicky at the idea that I should
have changed trains in Philadelphia and that we were headed back
again to New York City. I couldn't stand it any longer and,
summoning courage out of nowhere, I got off my cramped feet
towards the conductor, asking him with a terrific Spanish accent,
"Weel you pleaze tell mee where ees thees train goin' too?"
"W-H-O-A-T!", he barked at me.
I still remember his exclamation, which now would have seemed to
me more or less casual. At that time it sounded like a blast. With a
lump in my throat I repeated the question and the man answered
what to me seemed a couple of "blahs". Needless to say, I didn't

understand a single word, but nonetheless I thanked him ending my

words with a polite "sir". And very sheepishly I resumed my seat

hoping against hope that I were headed in the right direction. And I

was.

If I had not been so stubborn during my high school days, if I had

then realized the benefits and solace that are behind a bilingual

education, I would never have felt so worried and embarrassed as I

did feel that unforgettable night of my first trip to the Middle West.

And I would have felt more at ease and more like a human being

during the next ensuing months and even years. For Father Time

had already reserved for me a dreadful lesson: being called a

foreigner by those whose national congress bestowed on me the

citizenship common to them!

Then came the morning, my first morning in America. The waitress

at the counter asked me what I would like for breakfast –a question
whose import I could only guess. And I said, "coffee and bread,"
which is the typical breakfast of the Puerto Rican middle classes, or
so it was in those days. I could sense that something was going
wrong, for I didn't see any bread around but just rolls and at that time
I didn't even know if those things were edible at all! Nevertheless
less, she brought me rolls, which I found delicious and asked me in a
matter-of-fact way if I wanted milk or cream in my coffee. And
there I stumbled again! Down home it is all milk and nothing else
but milk, regardless of the fat contents of the stuff. So I said almost
in a whisper, "Yes, milk." And there she came back again with the
same question, "I didn't get you—cream or milk?"
Even today I don't know what that waitress finally put in my coffee.

It might have been milk or cream or even water for all I cared. I
downed my coffee with a couple of gulps and left the place as fast as
I could.
You will probably ask yourself why I should feel so embarrassed
about trifling incidents like those. It might perhaps require a lengthy
book to answer that seemingly unimportant question. I was already
beginning to see in my flesh and soul the likeness of the ordinary
American student, except for my dark brown eyes and my slightly
swarthy complexion. And although mine was a different racial
stock, it was dawning upon me that I was not here on charity, that as
an American citizen I was entitled to certain rights and immunities
and that was a student, which is always looked upon with utmost
kindness and sympathy, I was more or less entitled to the freedom of
the land.

But was I? Yes indeed! Wherever I went everybody met me with a
warm smile, everybody seemed to love me. But oh Lord, if I could
only correspond to their many niceties in precisely their vernacular!
And that was indeed out of the question for even if I somehow
subdued my terrible accent I still did not properly understand what
was being said around me. Why, oh why didn't I study more and
better English during my high school days! Although as I have said before, I and many fellows like me
considered it unpatriotic to cultivate the English language, the Puerto
Rican Department of Education is much to blame for this deficiency.
I know, and let it be here so consigned, that behind all these lies,
what seems an unfathomable pedagogical problem, for while some
proclaim that Spanish should be the medium of instruction in the
Puerto Rican public schools, other hold that if the Island is and for

many ears to come may remain under the American tutelage it is
only proper that most every subject be taught in the language of
Shakespeare, with a final aim at statehood. Be it as it may, the
classics should be less stressed in favor of a simple but intensive
course in conversational English. For, after all, when we study a
language we don't expect to become scholars but rather hope to be
understood by and to understand those who master it by the simple
expediency of their birth.
I'm not lying when I say that in my new life in Valparaiso even the
little things appealed to me. The succulent breakfasts, the coal in the
bins, the colorful sweaters, the sauerkraut, the fruit pies, they all
impressed me with the hue of the new and of the unknown.
Back home we don't know what real winter is. So we don't know of

the beauty of a frozen lake crowded with youthful and rhythmic
skaters; nor of the smooth ascent of a column of smoke from a brick
chimney in a gray winter morning; nor of the noiseless coasting of a
varnished sleigh; and least of all shall we ever realize how close one
gets to his Creator at the sight of the first ivory flakes descending in
an unsung symphony of silent glory!
We of the Spanish race generally take things for granted and lazily
make use of them just as they are. WE eat unscientifically and until
very recently didn't care much for a balanced diet. On the contrary, I
readily noticed when I first came up here that they didn't serve me
the same food in winter that they served me during the hot summer
months. They put special stress on fats during the winter season and
served plenty of salads and ice-tea during the summer. Things like
those which seemingly are unimportant draw a strong dividing line

between the health quotient and standard of living of the Americna
people and that of their South American counterpart.
Lounge or rest rooms all over the United States, especially in the
North are almost as neat and presentable as our own sitting parlors.
On the contrary, we are very careless at flushing our own sitting
stools and the lawn on our front gardens is generally unkempt. Is it
because we are truly lazy? I don't really think so. The trouble is that
we need to be re-educated from the bottom up, starting from the little
cares and niceties that really build up a highly civilized standard of
living such as the unique American standard. As a rule we are prone to scorn at the average American because he
has never heard of Baudelaire or because he thinks that Colombia is
a province of Argentine. We of the educated classes go very much

for intellectual sophistication. We love to
show off how much we
know about the classics and if we get together
drinking beer at a
parlor, it goes without saying that there will
be, going on for hours,
an exchange of pseudo-knowledge and an
unending recital of poems.
But just ask us about a minor motor trouble in
our car, if we own
one, or about a gadget in some machine, and
we just simply gape at
you only to drop the matter as one to be taken
care of by a common
artisan. Yet, in America these common
problems are well
understood and readily solved by your next
corner butcher or by
your nurse, or even by a high school
youngster or a bobby-soxer.
The average American town or city is
exceptionally clean. They say
that this is especially so in the North; but,
have you ever had a
chance to marvel at the neatness and
composure of the city of Tulsa,

whose white edifices and bungalows seem a
speck of foam amidst
the green Oklahoman pastures? Or have you
ever been to Miami,
whose pulchritude and neatness make it one of
the most outstanding
cities in the United States? Whether in a large
city or just a prairie
hamlet, you will always find in every corner a
box in the guise of a
big letter-drop with the inevitable inscription,
"Help keep our city
clean." And you can bet that from the smallest
tot to the eldest
patriarch in the community they will all
deposit in there from their
chewing gum wrapper to their torn newspaper.
In one of the big cities South of the border (I
will not say which for
fear of being mobbed,) the city council
recently established this
additional rubbish collecting system and it
broke my heart (my heart
that so often beats the American way,) to see
how young and old

folks alike neglected to avail themselves of the trash boxes
preferring the easy way –just drop their odds and ends on the
cracked side walks. Yes, cracked they are, for our public utility
services always remain at the end of the long-awaiting list of public
necessities to be taken care of by our illustrious aldermen!
In this country "the customer is always right" It is an inevitable
policy with clerks and owners of establishments catering to the
public to serve their very best and to see that the customer is always
satisfied. In our countries, believe it or not, it is almost the other
way around, whether or not it may work against the cash-register.
Our commercial slogan seems definitely to be, "take it or leave it."
And if you simply ask a waiter in a restaurant on a busy day if it
won't take long for your order to come, he will just tell you

nonchalantly that "he's only got two hands" meaning by that that he
cannot take care of everything at the same time. And since we are
used to those common impertinences, we just ignore them. The
American waiter or waitress, on the other hand, is courteous and
attentive, for, even if he or she were born in Greece or China or in
Peoria, the do have a profound sense of responsibility.
But if so happens in this democracy that the waiter who has served at
your table today may himself be waited on the day following and at
a classy restaurant at that. And his manners and social behavior will
never betray his humble occupation. Why? Because there are no
class barriers in this country; because a school education si
compulsory; because good manners are sort of standardized. In our
countries, however, my waiter shall never sit at my table, for once a

waiter always a waiter. It is a sort of stigma;
and it is invariably so
in our countries if you do not happen to
belong to the chosen few
who profess a classical career or who are well-
to – do.
When I first came to Valparaiso, Ind., I met a
Spanish fellow who
barely took up there an elementary course in
English and
mathematics. Twenty years later I met him
again in Chicago,
working as a bartender in the Pump House of
the Hotel Ambassador.
I thought to myself that there was a fellow
who had practically
accomplished nothing, for, while I was a
lawyer, he still was a bartender.
But how wrong I was! In tips alone he was
making more
than twenty dollars a day and besides the
thousands of dollars he had
already salted away he was owner of a big
apartment house in the
Windy City whose monthly rent alone netted
him around eighthundred

dollars. And he even retained an attorney to take care of his
legal matters! In fact, he was planning on retiring at the age of 45,
but-- business was still good! I know this is common day stuff to the
American reader, but the great majority of the foreign-born reader, I
am sure, will marvel at this simple statement of facts.
In my college days I needed money badly to pay my tuition fee and
other necessities, but I did not have the nerve to apply for a job
unless it were a white-collar position. There was Carlos Boero, a
Chilean fellow who studied mining engineering, and since we both
spoke the same language, we became very well acquainted with each
other. He was also poor but a sort of living exception to the no-work
Latin dogma. So one day he told me,
"Puerto Rico ---I went mostly by that name— let's get us a job here."

"Well, I need the money badly, but you know-
---there's no job we
can handle here."
"The hell there's none! We'll wash dishes."
"Heavens no! That's below our dignity.
Besides, what will
everybody say?"
There came up that eternal EVERYBODY so
common in our South
American countries. WE always think first of
how we will impress
our neighbors and what they will think about
us. And there is was,
washing dishes, of all things! Suppose they
knew back home? Even
my parents, mere mid-classers, would frown
at the idea.
But dishes I did, and believe me, I enjoyed it!
I count among the
happiest days of my life those in which, with a
long apron and a
coarse rag on my shoulder, I bent smilingly
over enormous pans of
water dipping the dishes while in sublimated
comradeship I
discussed the latest picture or the hard exams
with alluring flappers

and balloon-suited fellows of the roaring
twenties. Believe it or not,
my first real mixing with the American boys
and girls,
notwithstanding my terrible accent, took place
during the
apprenticeship of the unorthodox dish-
washing profession!
So I learned things the hard way, but a way
which is common to the
average struggling American student. On that
account these facts
may not impress the average American reader
but it surely will
impress the high hatted senoritas South of the
border whose silly
prejudice against all manual labor keeps them
within an isolated
kingdom of their own. A biased retirement
that makes them lose
contact with the true tempo of life and human
achievements, a
Shangri-la of self-imposed forgetfulness and
snobbishness that will
forever keep them ignorant of all progress as it
is planned and

achieved by the common, average man —that master-mind and

master-creator of this portentous country. When I first arrived in Valpo, as Valparaiso is called for short, I

wanted everyone to take notice that I was not a born American, that

my vernacular was not English and that I did not go for what I

thought were childish ideas, such as going to chapel, getting together

to discuss foot-ball and the like. Yet I had friends, lots of them,

because the American student is sympathetic and kind. Neither did I

let an opportunity go by without my telling the world, as I often did,

how tyrannical Uncle Sam was with little Puerto Rico.

The walls of my room in East Hall were literally plastered over with

Puerto Rican flags and pennants and I took pride at sticking on the

walls picture groups of beautiful senoritas so that everyone should

know that we were of true Spanish descent, as we are, and not a

bunch of mulattoes climbing up palm trees or peddling crabs and
bananas along pebbled streets. My blood just boiled ever so often
when a fellow-student, indeed with no malice aforethought, told me
that I didn't look like a Puerto Rican. Of course, right away I
realized that deep in their minds they clung to the idea that my
people were primitive half-breeds to say the least, exactly what they
had been told for generations in their history and geography books.
And again and again I told them that my island's black population,
numerically the the smallest black population throughout the West
Indies, is not over 25 percent, that we have splendid roads and
telephone and transportation and what not, ending it all with
unsavory remarks about Georgia and Alabama.
When I was in my second year, however, I began to care less and

less for my wall pennants and pictures and
little by little I
commenced to realize that there was an
increasing yearning in my
heart for the stars and stripes, for the
unchallenged beauty and
disposition of the American girls and for the
American way of
thinking and behaving.
Then I began to evade such questions as
where I was born, if I did
tango and fence and how I did like the U.S. A.
I did pretend with a
smile that I had forgotten all about it. Or
sometimes I would
jokingly say that I was born in Florida or
Texas.
I took pains at pronouncing my English words
with the least possible
accent and before I was going to say anything
no matter how trifling,
I rehearsed it mentally as fast as I could. I
begged of my closest
friends to correct my diction. I remember that
once in a restaurant I
asked a close friend to please pass me the
"butt-ter" and he laughed

and called me a damn foreigner. I asked him quite humbly how he
pronounced it and he said nonchalantly, "BORRAH, you fool!" He
came from Brooklyn. Well, anyway, I was quite steadfastly being
melted into the common caldron and I felt very proud about it too!
During a beautiful spring morning, strolling along Sager's Lake in
Valpo, I encountered a couple of kids not over seven years of age
and picked up a conversation with them. I asked them if they were
both going swimming, but I pronounced the word "both" with a
short "o." They laughed to their heart's content, repeating the word
out loud just as I had pronounced it. Young America was teaching
me how to speak English even thought I already knew a lot about
Milton and Shakespeare and Longfellow. I would have given
anything in the world to speak the language just like those kids

spoke it, even at the expense of my good-for-
nothing classics. I had
to content myself with the English that I
knew, with the English "as
she is spoke," Mark Twain fashion.
Once I said something about "powering"
(pouring) water from one
bucket into another and a friendly soul
corrected me. I have always
appreciated and in fact encouraged these
corrections for that is the
best way to learn a language. Experience has
taught me that in a
school room you merely learn how to WRITE
a language, but that
unless you go out on the street and venture
stumbling over your
words with the grocery man and the butcher
and the conductor, and,
yes of course, with your girl or boy friend,
you'll never learn how to
SPEAK it ---for languages are things much
alive and very
changeable. I boast of speaking some French,
learned in my school
days, but when it comes to understanding
what a Frenchman has to

say, unless he speaks very slowly, I am frankly at a loss. And even
though the menu or list is a thing mainly of French creation, once
when I was in Paris I almost sickened of malnutrition for all I could
order in the restaurants, to the waiter's understanding, was two eggs
"au plate!"
Indeed, languages are not only alive but changeable. Take for
instance those two daily "musts" of the American youngsters and
elders: the hamburger and the hot-dog. Twenty years ago everybody
accentuated their hamburgers on the second syllable while nowadays
the accent definitely goes on the first syllable, according to that most
orthodox of authorities, the people's unwritten dictionary. And
again, two decades ago in every corner of New York city you could
find hot-dogs or plain red-hots at your leisure. During La Guardia's

era, however, you cannot find the last survivor of that glorious

specimen. Of course, you will relish, if you like, on "frankfurter" on

a bun. They tell me that the well-bred little mayor banned the vulgar

word hot-dog from all stands, but, mind you, only to give way to a

longer word of dubious exotic meaning. I realize that I have somewhat departed from the true aim of this

work. Yet the above innuendos have a bearing on its prevailing

thought. For a man or woman who holler at a hero or at a baton-girl

in a Fourth-of-July parade with a mouthful of hot-dog undoubtedly

epitomizes a vigorous and youthful nation free of bias and worries.

Why should the American people or the millions of foreign born

citizens amalgamated with them worry about such daily problems as

abound in the rest of the world? There is no denying that they were

favored by plain good luck when they first settled in a country as vast and rich as theirs. But we have to admit that had it not been for

their courageous effort, they might at present still be struggling

along the borders of the original thirteen colonies, perhaps under the

British tutelage, with the great western plains still unconquered.

Take for instance, as a sad exemplary contrast, the republic of Brazil.

There is no question but that Brazil is a highly civilized nation, but

then again, her nationals seem to have written "finis" to her urban

and industrial expansion by simply dotting its Eastern coastline with

a few important cities and nothing more. I may be incurring the

enmity of many a South American, but I frankly assure that if the

American people, with their energetic resourcefulness and

practicality, would have landed on that enormous territory instead of

on Plymouth Rock, the whole world would have greatly benefited from the exploitation of the Amazonian Emporium.

The Americans truly chosen and privileged individuals, have not
contented themselves with merely exploiting what riches lie about
them in their homeland. They have taught China the art and science
of aviation, they have threaded the world with telephone lines
through the genial effort of the International Telephone & Telegraph
Corporation, they have installed heavy industrial machinery all over
Russia, turning the Russian farmer from a behind-the-horse plowed
into a machine-minded tiller of the soil, they have taught the world
how to can and conserve their food produce, how to live up to the
highest moral and physical standards, and, above all, how to live in
decent peace without fear of hunger or persecution.

If you live an honest and decent life, even if you are not an American

citizen, you will have in this country all the opportunities for which
you have always longed. You will be treated as one of them, with
rights and immunities. Whether you are a Jew, Black, Japanese, or a
Puerto Rican, your freedom of speech shall not be abridged, nor your
right to hold property, nor your right not to be unduly searched, nor
your right to worship God according to your own belief, nor, in
short, your constitutional privileges. Certain callings in this country have a sort of generally respected
priority among the nationals of certain countries. For instance,
laundries are generally owned by Chinese, dry-cleaning
establishments by Frenchmen, fruit peddling by Italian and coffee
pots and restaurants by Greeks. And, in the above given order, the
individual owners are invariably nick named by the average

American, Chan, Felix, Tony and Gus. But believe me, they are all
Americans in a sense, and they all struggle for and easily attain an
enviable economic security in the field of their pursuit.
Is the American immigration allotment just and wise? In my
opinion, definitely so. For if the barriers were indiscriminately lifted
for all sorts and numbers of immigrants, the country would be
stampeded by undesirable aliens and in such numbers that a surplus
of man-power would soon impoverish the land. The measure is not
only quantitative but qualitative in its beneficial import.
When I first arrived in New York City, about two decades ago, the
native American was really vanishing there. Along side-walks, in
the subway, in the movies, everywhere, one constantly heard Italian,
or Polish, or Spanish, or German, or French, but very little English

and broken at that. It was merely a necessary means of

communication among the enormous foreign-born population. But

twenty years after I was frankly intrigued at the all-English

conversations held throughout big cities such as New York, Chicago,

Philadelphia and New Orleans. Was it the alien that was vanishing

this time form the face of the country? The answer must be in the

negative. For although the older foreign-speaking generation still

roams at large, they speak nothing else but English while in public

and of course with their American-born off-spring, --the English they

were bound to learn during the past twenty years while the

immigration laws were bearing fruit. And, what is more, I have

noticed that the majority of foreigners have made it a habit to speak

only English among themselves.

A month or so ago I was in a restaurant in La Porte, Ind., with a
Puerto Rican friend and we were talking Spanish amongst ourselves.
The waitress overheard the conversation and asked us what
language we were speaking. I told her, but somewhat I noticed that
she herself spoke with an accent. Well, she was Greek, and her sister
beside her, also a waitress, was also born in the old country. But
they never spoke Greek amongst themselves because nowadays,
seemingly, it is a matter of bad taste to converse in a foreign
language in this country. Yes indeed, the melting pot is working fast;
and indeed yes, this country has not only and of long attained its
ethnological and linguistic unity but the same phenomenon has taken
place among the quarters of its foreign-born. When you first come to this country, you nurse ideas of an easy
conquest whether in the artistic, political or economical field. But

when you soon become aware of the true
pulsations of the American
hearts, of their utmost respect for their
neighbor's rights, their
hospitality and clean-cut manners and decency
you definitely change
and think and act like one of them. And when
in a matter of years
you bring over your brother or nephew again
to start like yourself
from the bottom of the ladder, you secretly
dislike him, for you have
already assimilated the American composure
and way of thinking.
This is truly a law-abiding people and on who,
while standing
wholeheartedly for your own rights, expect
the same reciprocity
from you. You can see that everyday,
everywhere. Take for
instance that all-American institution called
the public cafeteria.
They all act alike, disciplined like a martial
body. I've watched the
crowds entering cafeterias in New Your city,
in Miami, in Chicago,

in Galveston. They are like a sting of paper dolls patterned after the
same fashion, as keen and prompt as a double line of busy ants.
They act naturally but in a sort of mechanic way without ever
missing their objective—their tray and utensils and their favorite
courses. It seems as though they could just get in there blind-folded
without ever losing track of their objective. Why is it? They may
never have been in a particular cafeteria before, but, whether a Wac,
or a butcher or a lawyer, they are disciplined in their every move and
they know their way around without their once blinking an eye.
I have been to cafeterias with South American friends newly arrived
in this country and they all seem either clumsy or sophisticated.
They will pick their tray but will miss their soup spoon or their
napkin, and while they make up their mind as to what hot dish to

select, they have already missed the show, finding themselves at the
end of the counter with practically not a thing on their tray. And
then they strive at getting back on the line— all in vain, for the rush
of the hour and the vigilante spirit of the average American customer
will not let them get away with that. Or, they will just complain in
Spanish, yes, always in Spanish, even though they may speak good
English, about the vulgar atmosphere of the place and the poor
quality of the food – only to become cafeteria-minded after they
catch up with the routine months or years after.
It happened to me not so long ago. I was going from Chicago to
Miami and had to change buses in Jacksonville. Already it was a
long trip and there were still from eight to ten hours ahead of me
before I reached my final destination. I had a thick stub of a beard

and was tired and soiled and I knew I could not make the next bus
going into the deep South for there was a big crowd already standing
before the track. I thought I could get out of my predicament by
being smart and so I stealthily walked around the crowd and placed
myself between the chain and the bus, boldly handing over my ticket
to the driver. Not realizing my fraudulent ingenuity, the man was
going to punch my ticket when a woman from the crown=d yelled
with all her might,
"Who do you think you are? Get back in there you ---so and so!"
I still remember her, skinny and undersized, a half-pint sort of
creature, but defiant and energetic. The rest of the crowd began to
holler at me, demanding of the chauffeur that I be sent in back of the
line. I pleaded with the driver to please let me in, that I was tired
and had not slept a wind for a couple of night, and, finally, that I had

come a long ways—from Chicago. When the Southerner heard the
name of the Windy City his eyes closed to mere slits, his chest
actually expanded and his sense of responsibility sky-rocketed all of
a sudden, bursting into words like these, to the utmost satisfaction of
the booing crowd,
"From Chicago, eh? Then you should know better! Get back in
there!"
Needless to say, I blushed to the core of my head, got behind the
lengthy line and sheepishly awaited for the arrival of the next bus. I
finally made it but only after an hour and a half had elapsed from the
time I thought I was smart enough to break so fixed a rule! My
undisciplined Spanish blood had once more made a fool of myself!
Wherever you go in this country-- the post office, the movies, the
butcher's shop, the subway, the tax collector's office, it is a well

known matter of unwritten conventionality that you must keep in
line, no matter whether you are a law-enforcing officer or a
millionaire or even a lady. Just try and get ahead of the fellow
before you and —well, you couldn't even try, for they won't tolerate a
thing like that!
A nation as merry and youthful as these United States should never
lose it's leadership among the nations of the world. Before World
War II I visited London for a short while and the men and women
there close to middle-age impressed me as a very old folks, while the
youngsters, even in their teen-years seemed too matured and sad looking
for their age. Of course, the gloom of the ever-foggy
climate accounts in part for their behavior. But again, that was back
in the pre-depression years when life was plentiful and the British
merchant-marine mastered the seven seas. On the contrary, the

average American man and woman was and
ever seems to be happy
and youngish.
Go for once to Coney Island or to River view
Park, its Chicago
counterpart, and you will find there, mixed in
the joyful crowds, the
rosy-cheeked kid with the graying fellow,
everyone happy, everyone
care-free, eating pop-corn and drinking colas.
In our countries,
where our souls age so prematurely, it is
undignified for an elderly
gentleman to ride the merry-go-round even if
only to accompany his
children, or even to gnaw our hearts, however,
there is a secret
yearning for that sort of things, but they are
tabooed by silly
conventionalism.
In my country the so-called Commissioner of
Education, born in the
Island but reared in the continent, once took to
bike-riding while
holding office. You could hear the jokes and
satires about the old

fellow turned overnight into a school kid. Yet, in the States, I have

seen many a dignified college professor make use of that

invigorating means of locomotion without anyone ever making an

unpleasant remark about it.

Yes, we are an old-fashioned people. No man down the Rio Grande

would ever dare wear a colorful sports shirt on the streets as they so

commonly do up here. The least they would say about him is that he

was "queer." We are exceedingly particular about looking and acting

our own age, while the average American, simple and unaffected at

that, likes to look well groomed and youngish. If he goes to a beach

he likes to play ball and relax about the hot sands and even jump off

the spring board. We of the South, on the other hand, sit in a more of

less dignified position, as though we were dressed in tails instead of

a bathing suit, and are contented with conversing about business or

politics or with watching the younger
generation do its stuff. We are
certainly doomed by our own sophistication
and it is high time that
we revise the whole pattern of our
psychological behavior.
Although Americans are all scissored alike if
you want to dig into
the true nature of their stock just travel by bus.
Of course the
passenger next to you may be a Smith or a
Lowenstein or a Lopez or
a Kulikoff. But very soon after you start a
conversation with him or
her you will be calling him Vi or AL or Pat.
They hate formalities
and they make your trip pleasant and
congenial to your heart's
content. It is very unlikely that they will ask
you what your business
is or where you were born. They will just
discuss the weather and
the scenery and the last baseball score.
If it is during the summer time, your male
fellow travelers will

remove their coats and invite you to do the same; they will
inequitably be carrying a kit with safety-razor, tooth brush, tooth
paste and shaving cream, whether they are farmers or street sweepers
or businessmen. They will eat the same things at the bus depot
cafeteria, including the ever present bottle of grade A-1 milk. They
will be buying newspapers at every bus stop – for they are part of the
best informed people in the world. But even after a long journey and
a long conversation, don't expect them to exchange call card with
you, as a Latin would. You may have been anyone's seat companion
for twelve hours or a number of days and all he or she will tell you
upon leaving is, "Well, it's been nice to have known you," or simply,
"Happy landings!" You will never know who he or she really was
nor even the purpose of their long trip. A South American would

expect in a case like that a mutual survey of each others life and

business. And, at the end of the journey he will feel a little

sentimental about the inevitable separation. But in a country so big

as this, where buses and trains and planes are ever crowded and

people travel so often a polite smile will suffice at the termination of

our casual acquaintanceship. They will scoff at our excessive

politeness or rather at our racial moodiness if we show some concern

when the time comes to split apart. We of the South boast of being very hospitable. But let it be said

perhaps for the first time that our so called hospitality is nothing but

a pose. Time and again I have heard well-to-do matrons say in our

countries, when a beggar or someone in need knocks on their door,

that they are sorry there is nothing they can do about his plight. Or when the maid tells the master of the house that there is someone at

the door asking for food, the master very often says in a matter of

fact way, "Tell him that the master is not in." even though the leftovers

on his table are plentiful. Or if his next door neighbor happens

to drop in, he or his wife will frequently signal the maid that they are

not at home. In fact, if your visit bores them, which is quite often,

someone in the family will place a broom upside down behind a

door, without the visitor's awareness, of course, hoping that with that

ancestral hocus-pocus he will depart soon. I really don't know

where that sort of thing originated, but I remember too well that as a

did, I myself used to castigate our household broom in the above

fashion. We of the South frequently say that the "Americanos" do

not care for their neighbors in distress and that they let them starve

to death should they appeal to them for help. What a travesty of the
truth! I have seen many a housewife, especially during the
depression years, literally empty their refrigerators of cold meat cuts
and even eggs and sausages for a hungry hobo. And they even set a
table for him to eat, no matter how soiled his rags be. In like
circumstances, we would just give him a piece of stale bread or
perhaps a few pennies, or, if we are very charitable, we shall give
him a few left-overs in an old plate kept for such occasion, while the
poor fellow is supposed to down his meager meal while standing at
the rear entrance door. And when he is through eating, we matter of fact
expect him to say, "The Lord's blessings be with you!," as
though we were expecting something to the boot.
I have never seen a more kind-hearted people than the American

people. And I am not referring to their inborn softness as a nation,
nor to their quixotic lend-lease dealings as such but to their
individual and collective sympathy towards the hardships of their
fellow beings, be they white or black or yellow. Remember the did
that only recently was, according to medical science, doomed to die
on account of an incurable disease? And remember how the nation
was concerned about the tragic news, from Maine to California?
Remember the obscure lady who for days and months was struck
with severe hiccup and the President of the United States, in war
times, released a navy doctor from his Pacific duties commanding
him to fly back to the States to perform, as he did, a history making
operation on her? Remember the Broadway copper whose picture
appeared on the leading papers all over the nation only because he

was good natured enough to stop all traffic in order to let a mother
cat and her offspring cross the thoroughfare in safety? And the
private who was allowed to fly his general's plane to visit his dying
mother? And the so-called March of Dimes, and the President's
birthday balls to help the crippled, the have a heart movement,
the National War Fund, the Salvation Army, the YMCA,
the Red Cross, and –oh what's the use continuing! All these
simple gestures of a true citizenship and the names of these and
hundreds of other charitable institutions, are by themselves a
monument to the spirit of good-will and kindliness of the American
individual—a monument of longer standing than bronze and marble!
In the instance of the officer who flagged all traffic to stop, many of
my friends back home simply laughed at the "silly copper" for

showing such concern over an alley cat. And the way my friends felt
about the matter so felt my people. They really do not think much
about animals, especially marauding cats and dogs. And the boys of
the lower social stratum even kick and sling-shoot them about the
streets. On the contrary, the average American individual cares for
them a lot and shows greater concern if they look hungry and
helpless. I have seen an American lady in my native isle reprimand
a street peddler because he carried his fowls upside down, an act
punishable by law but about which our law enforcers do not seem to
care. Latin people cannot understand that sentimental gesture nor
can they conceive why the "Americanos" lavish so much money on
canned food for all sorts of pets and on hospitals for sick animals.
Only recently legal battles were fought in California in an endeavor

to save the life of a dog condemned to die because it killed it's
master's child. And the leading papers of the nation made of it a
front page issue. Back home they chuckled about the incident. You
can imagine what their reaction would be if they knew of the costly
monuments erected in Kentucky in memory of so many
thoroughbreds!
My race is moody and temperamental but to no practical or
meritorious end. To care for a sick dog may seem foolish in this
complex world –yet it shows kindness and mercy, without which the
national spirit may turn, in given psychological moments, to blood
shed and massacre. For if we do show pity towards the helpless
dumb creatures we will certainly behave in Christian-like manner in
the case of needful human beings.
In contrast to the above behavior, in our South Amercian countries a

cut-throat is a cut-throat, but once he is arraigned before a court of

justice, everybody feels pity towards him, and they all secretly wish

that he be given but a slight sentence. There is a horrible saying

South of the border attaining to murder cases, "el muerto al hoyo,"

literally, the dead to his grave. In other words, let the dead be

buried, let him rest in peace, but also let everyone more or less forget

about the dreadful homicide! Personally, although that all-Spanish

feeling is racially latent in my heart, I go for the American inflexible

way of imparting justice, and, of course, for the American

sympathetic mood towards the dumb creatures. In fact, not only

from a sentimental and straightforward stand but also from a rational

point of view that's the way it should always be.

Well, I could write pages and pages setting out instances like the above mentioned in an endeavor to definitely establish the

demarcation line between the psychological trends of the American

people on one hand and those of the people of my own race on the

other. I will give you the taste of a last example, in fact, the latest

one, which occurred in San Juan, the capital of Puerto Rico, long

after V-J day.

I was sipping beer in a public parlor with a number of friends when

all of a sudden a Puerto Rican soldier, just arrived from overseas

duties, literally batter-rammed a U. S. marine with his fists. After

the commotion was over and the M.P's showed up I was informed

that the source of the fight was that the marine, who evidently had

downed too much liquor, had remarked a few unsavory words about

the so-and-so Puerto Ricans. Everybody seemed proud about the soldier's gesture, except, of course, the poor marine and the M. P.'s.

But frankly, I felt thoroughly unhappy about the whole incident. If the marine said something out of place, due regard should be had of the fact that he was tipsy. Besides, his unfortunate remark, in the ears of a truly liberal-minded citizenry, should not be a matter of such deep concern, for the opinion of a carefree sailor can in no way change or debase the moral, racial and historical acquisitions of a people. In that sailor, no matter how distasteful his remarks might be, I only saw the symbol of the American youth who braved the mined sea-lanes so that you and I may live a decent and peaceful life devoid of hunger and fear and persecution. Sadly enough, my friends and the rest of the crowd in that beer parlor only saw in the lonely marine a loose-tongued foreigner disdainfully depicting their

fatherland. They ought to have been in
Chicago in V-J day, as I was,
to see how everyone acclaimed the soldier and
marines, no matter
how tipsy and unpleasant they might have
been and regardless of
what they said about their own Uncle Sam and
of the involuntary
servitude pertaining to the uniform. There is
such a tremendous lack
of understanding between the actual
generation of Puerto Ricans and
the American residents there, especially men
in uniform, that it is
imperative that the whole pattern of our
mutual relations be
thoroughly revised. Personally, I believe that
the deficiency should
be hunted out in the public school system and
in the official mania
for importing into the Island good-for-nothing
carpet-bagger whose
nonchalance is a definite source of irritation
and Angle-Phobia.
The same feeling of misapprehension exists in
many a South

American country against Uncle Sam's men in uniform. --Thousands
of Puerto Rican soldiers, wearing the same glorious khaki and just
arrived from the Canal Zone tell unpleasant stories about the
Panamanians despising them because while speaking the language
common to them, they, the Puerto Rican's, are mere serfs of a nation
that for half a century has enslaved their native isle. They nickname
them "Slaves" although they probably secretly envy their debonair
Martial and the trust placed on them while assigned to defend so
vital a spot as the Panama Canal.
But brushing aside those minor grudges against the "Northern
Colossus," for they are more or less politically biased, it remains a
fact that now more than ever the whole world is anxiously looking
forward to its moral and economic liberation through the help and
inspiration that emanates from America. The whole world was set

free from it's Axis bonds thanks to the far-
reaching vision of the
American statesmen and to the prodigious
industrial achievements of
this nation. And now the world, harassed and
crippled from a long
fastidious war, is slowly but steadily getting
back on it's feet through
the merciful lend-lease policy of this most
charitable and
enterprising nation of nations.
This, in short, is my humble tribute to
America. And with it goes my
invitation to all the foreigners living this side
of the Atlantic and to
those considering coming to it, to cast
overboard all sorts of
prejudices and all political creeds inconsistent
with the American
way of thinking, for the salvation of the
human soul and of well earned
patrimonies should not depend on the advent
of improvised
pragmatism's but rather on the patterns of the
American ideology

which has proved to be a symbol of moral strength and civil pulchritude.

CONCLUSION

It's been 67 years since my father's genuine message was written.
Simple gratitude was the driving force to thank our great nation for
the opportunities he'd never had—other than in this great land of
opportunity.
My father mentioned the all American traditions such as baseball,
bobby sox, hot dogs & ice cream. 67 years later, April 2013 the
Boston Marathon—another tradition synonymous with Americana,
was bombed.
What can we do to pull together and get this great country of ours
back on it's feet?!
Like my father's diverse background, our nations strength was built
on the cultural diversity of our people. I feel his message is
important because it is within that very diversity we need to weave

together towards a renewed patriotism that honors strength instead of
condoning a weak and liberal set of rules that allows the children of
our future to rebel. If America is to uphold the standard of the father
land, then before it's too late, we need to pull up our bootstraps and
learn from our greatest adversaries. I truly believe that our greatest
teachers ARE our greatest adversaries. They teach us what and
where our weaknesses lie. Each rebellion must not go in vain.
The rebellious teenager, with the help of our "soft" attitude has
turned into the spoiled brat. When children act up, the parent learns
different. Parents were not born with instructions, and our political
agendas too, --must change.
As paradoxical as it sounds, the very instrument that made this
country so desirable to all the Florentino's out there, needs to be
reformed. Although immigration is synonymous with "coming to

America" I believe it is long over due in which we place stricter
rules on immigration and it's laws. We must weed out those who
come to America for an Education degree and to make a lawful
living here, verses those with a distinct and volatile objection. I
would hope to see in my time, improved and stricter laws that still
encourage the American Dream.
My father obtained the American Dream with an overriding sense of
appreciation for what this country gave him. Unfortunately the
immigrants of today have become so used to entitlements, that we
are no longer dealing with the appreciative immigrant.

It is with sincere patriotism, pride and hope that my father's message be
understood by the Un-American.

ABOUT THE AUTHORS

Florentino "Tino" Prieto Azuar was born October 10, 1902, in Rincon, Puerto Rico. He was a lawyer and interim professor of law at the University of Puerto Rico in San Juan, and attended San Cristobal Catholic Church there. He graduated from Valparaiso School of law in Indiana and was a member of the American and Puerto Rican Bar Associations, Sigma Delta Kappa Law Fraternity and the Casa de Espana club in San Juan, P.R.

Suzanne Prieto Berry was born March 3, 1955 in San Juan, Puerto Rico. Graduated from Florida Southern College with a B.A. in Languages/Communications and studied at The University of Madrid, Spain. Authored the book: "Less is More" in 2012

www.ingramcontent.com/pod-product-compliance
Lightning Source LLC
Chambersburg PA
CBHW070749290526
45795CB00002B/531